The Nature of a Woman

Navigating Her 4 Week Mood Cycle

Workbook

The Nature of a Woman

Navigating Her 4 Week Mood Cycle

Workbook

Gary P. Simmons

SMASY PUBLISHING

Copyright 2017 Gary P. Simmons.
All rights reserved.

The content and ideas in this book belong to the author Gary P. Simmons.

You're welcome to learn and apply the ideas, however no part of this publication may be used, reproduced or shared in any form whatsoever without written permission from the publisher.

Limits of liability

The ideas, strategies, tactics and techniques in this book are of a general nature. I can't guarantee any specific outcomes. You should use common sense to ensure that this book is suitable and appropriate for your unique situation. Ultimately, you are responsible for your own results.

Any other questions?

If you have any questions, please contact the author via the publisher, Smasy Publishing. The contact information can be found at:

www.SmasyPublishing.com/contact-us

ISBN: 978-0-9752040-2-3

Dedication

This book is dedicated to all the women who taught me what they need from a partner. These many and varied experiences have allowed me to now have the relationships of my dreams.

Contents

Introduction 1
4 Week Mood Cycle Journal Instructions 3
The Plan of Attack 4
Important points 7
Getting Started 8
Example (step 1) 9
Example (step 2) 10
Week 1 11
Example (step 3) 14
Week 2 17
Week 3 21
Week 4 25
Week 5 29
Week 6 33
Week 7 37
Week 8 41
Week 9 45
Week 10 49
Week 11 53
Week 12 57
Mood Cycle Analysis Results 61
Example (step 4) 63
Moving Forward 68
Bonus Content 69
Resource Page 70
About the Author 71
Notes 72

Introduction

Relationship

"The way in which two or more people or things are connected."

Merriam-Webster Dictionary

This workbook has been designed to be used in conjunction with the 'Nature of a Woman: Navigating Her 4 week Mood Cycle' book or audiobook.

At this point, I'm assuming that you've either read or listened to this book and your now ready to take the next step in understanding how to improve your relationship.

If you haven't read the book or listened to the audiobook, you can access these resources by using this link: www.survivalskillsformen.com

In all relationships, it's inevitable that misunderstandings will be made by men and women. The real issue is how we deal with our mistakes and how we respond accordingly.

In the 'Nature of a Woman' book and audiobook, I address how men must take responsibility for the way in which they handle various situations and conflicts in relationships.

This workbook is for men who are serious about improving and developing their relationship. It's a tool to help you learn what you need to do, to assure that your partner feels loved, appreciated and secure throughout each phase of her 4 week mood cycle.

It's also a means for you to discover what your partner's questions, doubts, fears and insecurities are *really* all about.

Specifically, this workbook will help you to:

- Figure out exactly *when* your partner's distinctive mood cycles occur and how long each of the 4 phases last

- Understand her particular re-occurring questions, doubts, insecurities and fears about you and your relationship with her

- Prepare a kind, sensitive and meaningful response that can help you both address the issues that are causing stress

If you apply yourself to this process for a minimum of three cycles, you'll be able to anticipate what to expect in the weeks ahead. You'll become an expert in responding and working through your specific relationship issues, rather than being confused, frustrated and upset.

Through trial and error and with the assistance of my Nature of a Woman book or audiobook, you'll begin to see your partner's distinct pattern emerge. This will equip you to meet her needs during each phase of her mood cycle.

So, let's get to work!

4 Week Mood Cycle Journal Instructions

The workbook is set up to cover THREE 4 week mood cycles, a total of twelve weeks.

To achieve the best possible results:

- Read the Nature of a Woman book or listen to the audiobook

- Start your Mood Cycle Journal in Relief week

- Make notes in the corresponding sections of the journal about what you believe your partner is experiencing during her 4 week mood cycle

- Diligently continue for at least three complete cycles

- As you see a pattern emerge from her various mood states, note down some strategies. Also, note what you did or said that worked and what didn't

- At this point, you'll know how to best respond to her, as well as have the information necessary, to know what to say, when to say it and… how to say it.

The Plan of Attack

You have the option of utilizing your Mood Diary in two ways:

Option 1

This is the brief method. Use option 1 so you can get an *overview* of what's going on.

If you're not quite ready for a sustained and detailed examination of your relationship and you just want to gain some clarity by distinguishing the different phases of your partner's 4 week mood cycle, then it's best to utilize Option 1.

Step 1
Every evening make a note about what you've observed, particularly your partner's emotions. Place a tick in each of the 'Daily Review' boxes.

Step 2 (optional)
If you feel up to it, jot down some very brief notes and elaborate on your observations in the 'Daily Notes' (Happiness, Questions, Doubts, Fears and Issues) section.

Option 2

This option provides the means for you to begin a detailed analysis of your partner's moods and most importantly, your relationship as a whole.

It's a practical tool for you to gain insight into *exactly* what doubts, fears and insecurities your partner has, as they arise, as well as what triggers them - and when.

With this awareness, you can work on changing or improving how you respond to your partner and devise ways to best manage those re-occurring issues.

Keep in mind that knowing your partner and how you interact with her, gives you choices, which also makes option 2 an exercise in self empowerment for you.

Obviously, Option 2 is going to take more time, effort and vigilance to complete.

There's no doubt that making the commitment to work on 'Option 2' will be a process, a commitment and a challenge.

When the going gets tough, keep in mind that the object of this exercise, is to have a mutually enjoyable relationship and a happy and contented home life.

As is the case with anything that is worthwhile, if you put in the effort, you'll gain the clarity needed to achieve a great result.

It's totally up to you to decide on how you want to use your mood diary.

Maybe just start off by using Option 1 for a couple of cycles and then, when your confident, embark on Option 2.

The Steps For Utilising Option 2

Step 1

Every evening make a note about what you've observed is happening with your partner's emotions. Then, place a tick in each of the 'Daily Review' boxes.

Step 2

Jot down some very brief notes about *what* she's telling you and *why* you think she's saying these things in the Daily Notes (this is the 'Happiness, Questions, Doubts, Fears and Issues' section).

Step 3

Once per week, tabulate those feelings into the 'Weekly Note Summary' table.

Step 4

After dedicating time to your mood diary for three months, use the data you collected to formulate your partner's unique Mood Cycle Analysis.

Once you've completed the Mood Cycle Analysis, for all 4 phases of your partner's cycle, you'll know what's going on in your relationship.

The Mood Cycle Analysis, will help you see a distinct pattern emerge from the disarray and confusion surrounding your partner's fluctuating moods and emotions. It allows you to accurately predict *when* each phase of her 4 week mood cycle will begin, so you can prepare yourself accordingly.

With these insights about your partner and yourself, you can then work together to create the strategies, which can change the aspects of your relationship that are causing you both pain and frustration.

Bear in mind, that we ALL have negative and destructive patterns and that we are *all* a work in progress! So don't be afraid of being wrong or making mistakes.

What you are about to do is commendable. Most people live in denial, because they're in a perpetual state of emotional 'survival mode'.

It takes a lot of courage and vigilance to consciously make the effort to embark on this journey of relationship self discovery.

Only good can result from this exercise.

That's why I personally recommend that you dive in and start with option 2.

Important points

- Value your relationship enough to see this project all the way through!

- The best time to work on your mood diary, is when you have a quiet space to consider your relationship and your feelings, perhaps before bed.

- *Consistency* is the key. It WILL take some effort to do this every single day for three cycles. It may be difficult sometimes, especially when you're feeling tired. Don't give up! This is when you need determination and self discipline. Remind yourself that it only takes a few minutes to enter your data… she's worth it!

- Don't over analyze what you write down. Just briefly document your observations and keep it simple. Remember, you're the only one reading this.

- Open the page at step 1) tick as many boxes that are relevant for you on that day.

- If you are working with option 2, go straight to step 2) and quickly jot down the first thing that comes into your mind.

- On day 7 or when you realize that she's shifted into the next phase of her cycle, allow a few extra minutes for step 3, so you can fill out the 'Weekly Note Summary'.

Before you get started with Step 1, as well as the other steps, have a look at my example so you can get an idea of how it all works. As I mentioned above, don't analyze your thoughts. Rather, trust your gut feelings and just tick the relevant sections.

Remember, you can't make a mistake here.

A Word of Caution

Wait until you have documented at least THREE 4 week cycles before you begin to initiate a conversation about mood cycles, PMS or any other menstrual cycle related issues.

If you discuss this too early, your observations will likely get shot down in flames. However, once you've completed your three cycle analysis, you will have some hard evidence as well as irrefutable proof that you know what you're talking about.

Then it's all about communication, which is addressed in The Nature of a Woman book and audiobook.

Getting Started

It's important to begin this journaling process when your partner moves into Relief Week.

Although it may be tempting to start in Volcano week, when she's more volatile than usual, bide your time and standby.

If you're reluctant to ask her if she's menstruating, look for the clues that I discuss in The Nature of a Woman book or audiobook.

Another tip before you start journaling each day or evening, is to try this calming and mind clearing breathing exercise.

- Slowly and gently breathe in through your nose and then slowly out through your mouth, as if through a straw.

- As you slowly exhale, purse your lips to make a small opening to release the breath. Exhale completely.

- Repeat this 5-8 times.

Now you're ready to begin.

Note:
To help you develop this breathing technique I've included a link to a free audio lesson. You can find the link in the Bonus Content chapter.

Example (step 1)

Daily Review - Cycle 1: Week 1 - RELIEF Week (example)

Start Date: 01/23/2009

Tick the box that best relates to what you have observed about your partner, in as many of the category boxes below as you need.

<u>What mood state did you observe in your partner today?</u>

Feelings	Day 1	Day 2	Day 3	Day 4	Day 5	Day 6	Day 7
Joyful							
Happy				√			√
Contented							
Insightful						√	
Neutral		√	√	√	√		
Sad	√						
Anxious							
Frustrated	√						
Overwhelmed							
Doubtful							
Worried	√						
Discouraged							
Exhausted		√	√				
Anger							
Despair							
Numb							

<u>How did she feel about you today?</u>

Feelings	Day 1	Day 2	Day 3	Day 4	Day 5	Day 6	Day 7
Love							
Passion							
Contentment							
Secure						√	√
Optimism							√
Neutral		√	√	√	√		
Boredom							
Frustration	√						
Anger							
Insecurity	√						
Suspicious							
Hatred/Rage							

Example (step 2)

Happiness, Questions, Doubts, Fears & Issues

Discreetly watch and listen to your partner. Make some brief notes about what she is saying and when. Each evening before you go to bed write down what she's happy about or note the questions, doubts, fears and issues that are weighing on her mind.

To help you gain some clarity about her feelings and emotions, also elaborate a little on what you put in your 'Daily Review' in Step 1.

Before you get started, here's an example from my Mood Diary.

Day 1: (example)   During the lead up to her period she seemed quite insecure and I felt she was taking things out on me. I saw a shift today though. Things are calmer and I can sense some feelings of guilt. I feel Christine is making a conscious effort to be kind to me today. I still think we've both been feeling a little shell shocked today though, so things still feel a little strained.

Day 2: (example)   A much better day to day. Christine started off feeling frustrated with life in general. After breakfast I suggested that since it was Sunday we should take a walk together. It was also great to see her take some time to do some Yoga today.

Week 1

RELIEF Week - Cycle 1.

Daily Review: Week 1

Cycle 1: Week 1 - RELIEF Week

Start Date: ....

Tick the box that best relates to what you have observed about your partner, in as many of the category boxes below as you need.

What mood state did you observe in your partner today?

Feelings	Day 1	Day 2	Day 3	Day 4	Day 5	Day 6	Day 7
Joyful							
Happy							
Contented							
Insightful							
Neutral							
Sad							
Anxious							
Frustrated							
Overwhelmed							
Doubtful							
Worried							
Discouraged							
Exhausted							
Anger							
Despair							
Numb							

How did she feel about you today?

Feelings	Day 1	Day 2	Day 3	Day 4	Day 5	Day 6	Day 7
Love							
Passion							
Contentment							
Secure							
Optimism							
Neutral							
Boredom							
Frustration							
Anger							
Insecurity							
Suspicious							
Hatred/Rage							

Daily Notes: Week 1

Cycle 1: Week 1 - RELIEF Week

Happiness, Questions, Doubts, Fears & Issues

Discreetly watch and listen to your partner. Make some brief notes about what she is saying and when. Each evening before you go to bed write down what she's happy about or note the questions, doubts, fears and issues that are weighing on her mind.

To help you gain some clarity about her feelings and emotions, also elaborate a little on what you put in your 'Daily Review' in Step 1. If you need more space use the 'notes' pages at the end of the book.

Day 1: ....
....

Day 2: ....
....

Day 3: ....
....

Day 4: ....
....

Day 5: ....
....

Day 6: ....
....

Day 7: ....
....

After day 7 or when you feel she's shifted into the next phase, tabulate your notes in the Weekly Note Summary

Other Points: ....
....

Example (step 3)

Weekly Note Summary

It's now time to tabulate your results.

At the end of each phase, examine your 'Daily Review' entries from the entire week from Step 1, as well as your notes in Step 2.

The following pages are set up to represent one phase of your partner's 4 week mood cycle.

Since this Mood Diary has been designed to be used over three cycles or three months, you'll find that there are three tables in a row which represent all of the phases that you've documented over this period. For example, the tables are listed as follows:

- The first table is for 'Cycle 1 - Week 1' (her 1st Relief week)
- The second table is for 'Cycle 2 - Week 5' (her 2nd Relief week)
- The third table is 'Cycle 3 - Week 9' (her 3rd Relief week)

All the phases Relief Week, Love Week, Restless Week and Volcano Week are listed in this way.

On day seven of each phase/week or when you've noticed her move into the next phase of her mood cycle, review your entries from the past week and write down the main points into the 'Weekly Summary' table. Also, add in the key issues that you've noted about your partner from Steps 1 & 2.

Hang in there! This step consolidates 3 months worth of your important data and puts it all in one place, so you can utilize it a little later on.

Also, use these weekly tables to calculate how long each of your partner's phases last for, so you can work out an average number of days that she spends in each of them.

As you get more familiar with the duration of each phase within your partner's cycle it will be far easier to predict how she'll feel hormonally on any given week.

Here's an example from my Mood Diary so you'll know how to do it.

RELIEF Week - Cycle 1 (example)

Start date: 01/23/2009 End date: 01/30/2009

Day	Observations about your partner and her feelings towards you	Other issues (if any)
1	Very frustrated with me. She's quite hostile and I'm in her 'bad books'	Worried about finances
2	A better mood than yesterdays, although she's still distant.	Still talking about finances
3	A much better day! Definitely more affectionate.	We shared some laughs
4	She's friendly but I feel I've been kept at arms length	Still a bit distant
5	I've noticed she's reaching out to her girlfriends. Asked me to cook	She's pointing out what she's done
6	Wanted to hang out with me today. She's quite affectionate	Still talking about money issues
7	Was pleased and grateful when I offered to cook dinner and wash up	We had a great day

Weekly Note Summary: Week 1

RELIEF Week - Cycle 1

Start date:.................................... End date:....................................

Day	Observations about your partner and her feelings towards you	Other issues (if any)
1		
2		
3		
4		
5		
6		
7		

Week 2

LOVE Week - Cycle 1.

Daily Review: Week 2

Cycle 1: Week 2 - LOVE Week

Start Date: ....

Tick the box that best relates to what you have observed about your partner, in as many of the category boxes below as you need.

<u>What mood state did you observe in your partner today?</u>

Feelings	Day 1	Day 2	Day 3	Day 4	Day 5	Day 6	Day 7
Joyful							
Happy							
Contented							
Insightful							
Neutral							
Sad							
Anxious							
Frustrated							
Overwhelmed							
Doubtful							
Worried							
Discouraged							
Exhausted							
Anger							
Despair							
Numb							

<u>How did she feel about you today?</u>

Feelings	Day 1	Day 2	Day 3	Day 4	Day 5	Day 6	Day 7
Love							
Passion							
Contentment							
Secure							
Optimism							
Neutral							
Boredom							
Frustration							
Anger							
Insecurity							
Suspicious							
Hatred/Rage							

Daily Notes: Week 2

Cycle 1: Week 2 – LOVE Week

Happiness, Questions, Doubts, Fears & Issues

Discreetly watch and listen to your partner. Make some brief notes about what she is saying and when. Each evening before you go to bed write down what she's happy about or note the questions, doubts, fears and issues that are weighing on her mind.

To help you gain some clarity about her feelings and emotions, also elaborate a little on what you put in your 'Daily Review' in Step 1. If you need more space use the 'notes' pages at the end of the book.

Day 1: ....

....

Day 2: ....

....

Day 3: ....

....

Day 4: ....

....

Day 5: ....

....

Day 6: ....

....

Day 7: ....

....

After day 7 or when you feel she's shifted into the next phase, tabulate your notes in the Weekly Note Summary

Other Points: ....

....

Weekly Note Summary: Week 2

LOVE Week - Cycle 1

Start date:.................................... End date:....................................

Day	Observations about your partner and her feelings towards you	Other issues (if any)
1		
2		
3		
4		
5		
6		
7		

Week 3

RESTLESS Week - Cycle 1.

Daily Review: Week 3

Cycle 1: Week 3 - RESTLESS Week

Tick the box that best relates to what you have observed about your partner, in as many of the category boxes below as you need.

What mood state did you observe in your partner today?

Feelings	Day 1	Day 2	Day 3	Day 4	Day 5	Day 6	Day 7
Joyful							
Happy							
Contented							
Insightful							
Neutral							
Sad							
Anxious							
Frustrated							
Overwhelmed							
Doubtful							
Worried							
Discouraged							
Exhausted							
Anger							
Despair							
Numb							

How did she feel about you today?

Feelings	Day 1	Day 2	Day 3	Day 4	Day 5	Day 6	Day 7
Love							
Passion							
Contentment							
Secure							
Optimism							
Neutral							
Boredom							
Frustration							
Anger							
Insecurity							
Suspicious							
Hatred/Rage							

Daily Notes: Week 3

Cycle 1: Week 3 – RESTLESS Week

Happiness, Questions, Doubts, Fears & Issues

Discreetly watch and listen to your partner. Make some brief notes about what she is saying and when. Each evening before you go to bed write down what she's happy about or note the questions, doubts, fears and issues that are weighing on her mind.

To help you gain some clarity about her feelings and emotions, also elaborate a little on what you put in your 'Daily Review' in Step 1. If you need more space use the 'notes' pages at the end of the book.

Day 1: ....

....

Day 2: ....

....

Day 3: ....

....

Day 4: ....
......

....

Day 5: ....

....

Day 6: ....

....

Day 7: ....

....

After day 7 or when you feel she's shifted into the next phase, tabulate your notes in the Weekly Note Summary

Other Points: ....

....

Weekly Note Summary: Week 3

RESTLESS Week - Cycle 1

Start date:.................................. End date:..................................

Day	Observations about your partner and her feelings towards you	Other issues (if any)
1		
2		
3		
4		
5		
6		
7		

Week 4

VOLCANO Week - Cycle 1.

Daily Review: Week 4

Cycle 1: Week 4 - VOLCANO Week

Start Date: ....

Tick the box that best relates to what you have observed about your partner, in as many of the category boxes below as you need.

What mood state did you observe in your partner today?

Feelings	Day 1	Day 2	Day 3	Day 4	Day 5	Day 6	Day 7
Joyful							
Happy							
Contented							
Insightful							
Neutral							
Sad							
Anxious							
Frustrated							
Overwhelmed							
Doubtful							
Worried							
Discouraged							
Exhausted							
Anger							
Despair							
Numb							

How did she feel about you today?

Feelings	Day 1	Day 2	Day 3	Day 4	Day 5	Day 6	Day 7
Love							
Passion							
Contentment							
Secure							
Optimism							
Neutral							
Boredom							
Frustration							
Anger							
Insecurity							
Suspicious							
Hatred/Rage							

Daily Notes: Week 4

Cycle 1: Week 4 – VOLCANO Week

Happiness, Questions, Doubts, Fears & Issues

Discreetly watch and listen to your partner. Make some brief notes about what she is saying and when. Each evening before you go to bed write down what she's happy about or note the questions, doubts, fears and issues that are weighing on her mind.

To help you gain some clarity about her feelings and emotions, also elaborate a little on what you put in your 'Daily Review' in Step 1. If you need more space use the 'notes' pages at the end of the book.

Day 1: ....

....

Day 2: ....

....

Day 3: ....

....

Day 4: ....

....

Day 5: ....

....

Day 6: ....

....

Day 7: ....

....

After day 7 or when you feel she's shifted into the next phase, tabulate your notes in the Weekly Note Summary

Other Points: ....

....

Weekly Note Summary: Week 4

VOLCANO Week - Cycle 1

Start date:.................................... End date:....................................

Day	Observations about your partner and her feelings towards you	Other issues (if any)
1		
2		
3		
4		
5		
6		
7		

Week 5

RELIEF Week - Cycle 2.

Daily Review: Week 5

Cycle 2: Week 1 - RELIEF Week

Start Date: ....

Tick the box that best relates to what you have observed about your partner, in as many of the category boxes below as you need.

<u>What mood state did you observe in your partner today?</u>

Feelings	Day 1	Day 2	Day 3	Day 4	Day 5	Day 6	Day 7
Joyful							
Happy							
Contented							
Insightful							
Neutral							
Sad							
Anxious							
Frustrated							
Overwhelmed							
Doubtful							
Worried							
Discouraged							
Exhausted							
Anger							
Despair							
Numb							

<u>How did she feel about you today?</u>

Feelings	Day 1	Day 2	Day 3	Day 4	Day 5	Day 6	Day 7
Love							
Passion							
Contentment							
Secure							
Optimism							
Neutral							
Boredom							
Frustration							
Anger							
Insecurity							
Suspicious							
Hatred/Rage							

Daily Notes: Week 5

Cycle 2: Week 1 - RELIEF Week

Happiness, Questions, Doubts, Fears & Issues

Discreetly watch and listen to your partner. Make some brief notes about what she is saying and when. Each evening before you go to bed write down what she's happy about or note the questions, doubts, fears and issues that are weighing on her mind.

To help you gain some clarity about her feelings and emotions, also elaborate a little on what you put in your 'Daily Review' in Step 1. If you need more space use the 'notes' pages at the end of the book.

Day 1: ....

....

Day 2: ....

....

Day 3: ....

....

Day 4: ....

....

Day 5: ....

....

Day 6: ....

....

Day 7: ....

....

After day 7 or when you feel she's shifted into the next phase, tabulate your notes in the Weekly Note Summary

Other Points: ....

....

Weekly Note Summary: Week 5

RELIEF Week - Cycle 2

Start date:................................ End date:................................

Day	Observations about your partner and her feelings towards you	Other issues (if any)
1		
2		
3		
4		
5		
6		
7		

Week 6

LOVE Week - Cycle 2.

Daily Review: Week 6

Cycle 2: Week 2 - LOVE Week

Start Date: ....

Tick the box that best relates to what you have observed about your partner, in as many of the category boxes below as you need.

<u>What mood state did you observe in your partner today?</u>

Feelings	Day 1	Day 2	Day 3	Day 4	Day 5	Day 6	Day 7
Joyful							
Happy							
Contented							
Insightful							
Neutral							
Sad							
Anxious							
Frustrated							
Overwhelmed							
Doubtful							
Worried							
Discouraged							
Exhausted							
Anger							
Despair							
Numb							

<u>How did she feel about you today?</u>

Feelings	Day 1	Day 2	Day 3	Day 4	Day 5	Day 6	Day 7
Love							
Passion							
Contentment							
Secure							
Optimism							
Neutral							
Boredom							
Frustration							
Anger							
Insecurity							
Suspicious							
Hatred/Rage							

Daily Notes: Week 6

Cycle 2: Week 2 – LOVE Week

Happiness, Questions, Doubts, Fears & Issues

Discreetly watch and listen to your partner. Make some brief notes about what she is saying and when. Each evening before you go to bed write down what she's happy about or note the questions, doubts, fears and issues that are weighing on her mind.

To help you gain some clarity about her feelings and emotions, also elaborate a little on what you put in your 'Daily Review' in Step 1. If you need more space use the 'notes' pages at the end of the book.

Day 1: ....
....

Day 2: ....
....

Day 3: ....
....

Day 4: ....
....

Day 5: ....
....

Day 6: ....
....

Day 7: ....
....

After day 7 or when you feel she's shifted into the next phase, tabulate your notes in the Weekly Note Summary

Other Points: ....
....

Weekly Note Summary: Week 6

LOVE Week - Cycle 2

Start date:.............................. End date:..............................

Day	Observations about your partner and her feelings towards you	Other issues (if any)
1		
2		
3		
4		
5		
6		
7		

Week 7

RESTLESS Week - Cycle 2.

Daily Review: Week 7

Cycle 2: Week 3 - RESTLESS Week

Start Date: ....

Tick the box that best relates to what you have observed about your partner, in as many of the category boxes below as you need.

<u>What mood state did you observe in your partner today?</u>

Feelings	Day 1	Day 2	Day 3	Day 4	Day 5	Day 6	Day 7
Joyful							
Happy							
Contented							
Insightful							
Neutral							
Sad							
Anxious							
Frustrated							
Overwhelmed							
Doubtful							
Worried							
Discouraged							
Exhausted							
Anger							
Despair							
Numb							

<u>How did she feel about you today?</u>

Feelings	Day 1	Day 2	Day 3	Day 4	Day 5	Day 6	Day 7
Love							
Passion							
Contentment							
Secure							
Optimism							
Neutral							
Boredom							
Frustration							
Anger							
Insecurity							
Suspicious							
Hatred/Rage							

Daily Notes: Week 7

Cycle 2: Week 3 – RESTLESS Week

Happiness, Questions, Doubts, Fears & Issues

Discreetly watch and listen to your partner. Make some brief notes about what she is saying and when. Each evening before you go to bed write down what she's happy about or note the questions, doubts, fears and issues that are weighing on her mind.

To help you gain some clarity about her feelings and emotions, also elaborate a little on what you put in your 'Daily Review' in Step 1. If you need more space use the 'notes' pages at the end of the book.

Day 1: ....

Day 2: ....

Day 3: ....

Day 4: ....

Day 5: ....

Day 6: ....

Day 7: ....

After day 7 or when you feel she's shifted into the next phase, tabulate your notes in the Weekly Note Summary

Other Points: ....

Weekly Note Summary: Week 7

RESTLESS Week - Cycle 2

Start date:................................ End date:................................

Day	Observations about your partner and her feelings towards you	Other issues (if any)
1		
2		
3		
4		
5		
6		
7		

Week 8

VOLCANO Week - Cycle 2.

Daily Review: Week 8

Cycle 2: Week 4 - VOLCANO Week

Start Date: ....

Tick the box that best relates to what you have observed about your partner, in as many of the category boxes below as you need.

What mood state did you observe in your partner today?

Feelings	Day 1	Day 2	Day 3	Day 4	Day 5	Day 6	Day 7
Joyful							
Happy							
Contented							
Insightful							
Neutral							
Sad							
Anxious							
Frustrated							
Overwhelmed							
Doubtful							
Worried							
Discouraged							
Exhausted							
Anger							
Despair							
Numb							

How did she feel about you today?

Feelings	Day 1	Day 2	Day 3	Day 4	Day 5	Day 6	Day 7
Love							
Passion							
Contentment							
Secure							
Optimism							
Neutral							
Boredom							
Frustration							
Anger							
Insecurity							
Suspicious							
Hatred/Rage							

Daily Notes: Week 8

Cycle 2: Week 4 – VOLCANO Week

Happiness, Questions, Doubts, Fears & Issues

Discreetly watch and listen to your partner. Make some brief notes about what she is saying and when. Each evening before you go to bed write down what she's happy about or note the questions, doubts, fears and issues that are weighing on her mind.

To help you gain some clarity about her feelings and emotions, also elaborate a little on what you put in your 'Daily Review' in Step 1.

Day 1: ....
....

Day 2: ....
....

Day 3: ....
....

Day 4: ....
....

Day 5: ....
....

Day 6: ....
....

Day 7: ....
....

After day 7 or when you feel she's shifted into the next phase, tabulate your notes in the Weekly Note Summary

Other Points: ....
....

Weekly Note Summary: Week 8

VOLCANO Week - Cycle 2

Start date:................................ End date:................................

Day	Observations about your partner and her feelings towards you	Other issues (if any)
1		
2		
3		
4		
5		
6		
7		

Week 9

RELIEF Week - Cycle 3.

Daily Review: Week 9

Cycle 3: Week 1 - RELIEF Week

Start Date: ....

Tick the box that best relates to what you have observed about your partner, in as many of the category boxes below as you need.

<u>What mood state did you observe in your partner today?</u>

Feelings	Day 1	Day 2	Day 3	Day 4	Day 5	Day 6	Day 7
Joyful							
Happy							
Contented							
Insightful							
Neutral							
Sad							
Anxious							
Frustrated							
Overwhelmed							
Doubtful							
Worried							
Discouraged							
Exhausted							
Anger							
Despair							
Numb							

<u>How did she feel about you today?</u>

Feelings	Day 1	Day 2	Day 3	Day 4	Day 5	Day 6	Day 7
Love							
Passion							
Contentment							
Secure							
Optimism							
Neutral							
Boredom							
Frustration							
Anger							
Insecurity							
Suspicious							
Hatred/Rage							

Daily Notes: Week 9

Cycle 3: Week 1 - RELIEF Week

Happiness, Questions, Doubts, Fears & Issues

Discreetly watch and listen to your partner. Make some brief notes about what she is saying and when. Each evening before you go to bed write down what she's happy about or note the questions, doubts, fears and issues that are weighing on her mind.

To help you gain some clarity about her feelings and emotions, also elaborate a little on what you put in your 'Daily Review' in Step 1. If you need more space use the 'notes' pages at the end of the book.

Day 1: ....

....

Day 2: ....

....

Day 3: ....

....

Day 4: ....

....

Day 5: ....

....

Day 6: ....

....

Day 7: ....

....

After day 7 or when you feel she's shifted into the next phase, tabulate your notes in the Weekly Note Summary

Other Points: ....

....

Weekly Note Summary: Week 9

RELIEF Week - Cycle 3

Start date:................................ End date:................................

Day	Observations about your partner and her feelings towards you	Other issues (if any)
1		
2		
3		
4		
5		
6		
7		

Week 10

LOVE Week - Cycle 3.

Daily Review: Week 10

Cycle 3: Week 2 - LOVE Week

Start Date: ....

Tick the box that best relates to what you have observed about your partner, in as many of the category boxes below as you need.

<u>What mood state did you observe in your partner today?</u>

Feelings	Day 1	Day 2	Day 3	Day 4	Day 5	Day 6	Day 7
Joyful							
Happy							
Contented							
Insightful							
Neutral							
Sad							
Anxious							
Frustrated							
Overwhelmed							
Doubtful							
Worried							
Discouraged							
Exhausted							
Anger							
Despair							
Numb							

<u>How did she feel about you today?</u>

Feelings	Day 1	Day 2	Day 3	Day 4	Day 5	Day 6	Day 7
Love							
Passion							
Contentment							
Secure							
Optimism							
Neutral							
Boredom							
Frustration							
Anger							
Insecurity							
Suspicious							
Hatred/Rage							

Daily Notes: Week 10

Cycle 3: Week 2 – LOVE Week

Happiness, Questions, Doubts, Fears & Issues

Discreetly watch and listen to your partner. Make some brief notes about what she is saying and when. Each evening before you go to bed write down what she's happy about or note the questions, doubts, fears and issues that are weighing on her mind.

To help you gain some clarity about her feelings and emotions, also elaborate a little on what you put in your 'Daily Review' in Step 1. If you need more space use the 'notes' pages at the end of the book.

Day 1: ....

....

Day 2: ....

....

Day 3: ....

....

Day 4: ....

....

Day 5: ....

....

Day 6: ....

....

Day 7: ....

....

After day 7 or when you feel she's shifted into the next phase, tabulate your notes in the Weekly Note Summary

Other Points: ....

....

Weekly Note Summary: Week 10

LOVE Week - Cycle 3

Start date:.................................. End date:..................................

Day	Observations about your partner and her feelings towards you	Other issues (if any)
1		
2		
3		
4		
5		
6		
7		

Week 11

RESTLESS Week - Cycle 3.

Daily Review: Week 11

Cycle 3: Week 3 - RESTLESS Week

Start Date: ....

Tick the box that best relates to what you have observed about your partner, in as many of the category boxes below as you need.

Tick the box that best relates to what you have observed about your partner, in as many of the category boxes below as you need.

<u>What mood state did you observe in your partner today?</u>

Feelings	Day 1	Day 2	Day 3	Day 4	Day 5	Day 6	Day 7
Joyful							
Happy							
Contented							
Insightful							
Neutral							
Sad							
Anxious							
Frustrated							
Overwhelmed							
Doubtful							
Worried							
Discouraged							
Exhausted							
Anger							
Despair							
Numb							

<u>How did she feel about you today?</u>

Feelings	Day 1	Day 2	Day 3	Day 4	Day 5	Day 6	Day 7
Love							
Passion							
Contentment							
Secure							
Optimism							
Neutral							
Boredom							
Frustration							
Anger							
Insecurity							
Suspicious							
Hatred/Rage							

Daily Notes: Week 11

Cycle 3: Week 3 – RESTLESS Week

Happiness, Questions, Doubts, Fears & Issues

Discreetly watch and listen to your partner. Make some brief notes about what she is saying and when. Each evening before you go to bed write down what she's happy about or note the questions, doubts, fears and issues that are weighing on her mind.

To help you gain some clarity about her feelings and emotions, also elaborate a little on what you put in your 'Daily Review' in Step 1. If you need more space use the 'notes' pages at the end of the book.

Day 1: ....

....

Day 2: ....

....

Day 3: ....

....

Day 4: ....

....

Day 5: ....

....

Day 6: ....

....

Day 7: ....

....

After day 7 or when you feel she's shifted into the next phase, tabulate your notes in the Weekly Note Summary

Other Points: ....

....

Weekly Note Summary: Week 11

RESTLESS Week - Cycle 3

Start date:.................................... End date:..

Day	Observations about your partner and her feelings towards you	Other issues (if any)
1		
2		
3		
4		
5		
6		
7		

Week 12

VOLCANO Week - Cycle 3.

Daily Review: Week 12

Cycle 3: Week 4 - VOLCANO Week

Start Date: ....

Tick the box that best relates to what you have observed about your partner, in as many of the category boxes below as you need.

<u>What mood state did you observe in your partner today?</u>

Feelings	Day 1	Day 2	Day 3	Day 4	Day 5	Day 6	Day 7
Joyful							
Happy							
Contented							
Insightful							
Neutral							
Sad							
Anxious							
Frustrated							
Overwhelmed							
Doubtful							
Worried							
Discouraged							
Exhausted							
Anger							
Despair							
Numb							

<u>How did she feel about you today?</u>

Feelings	Day 1	Day 2	Day 3	Day 4	Day 5	Day 6	Day 7
Love							
Passion							
Contentment							
Secure							
Optimism							
Neutral							
Boredom							
Frustration							
Anger							
Insecurity							
Suspicious							
Hatred/Rage							

Daily Notes: Week 12

Cycle 3: Week 4 – VOLCANO Week

Happiness, Questions, Doubts, Fears & Issues

Discreetly watch and listen to your partner. Make some brief notes about what she is saying and when. Each evening before you go to bed write down what she's happy about or note the questions, doubts, fears and issues that are weighing on her mind.

To help you gain some clarity about her feelings and emotions, also elaborate a little on what you put in your 'Daily Review' in Step 1. If you need more space use the 'notes' pages at the end of the book.

Day 1: _____

_____

Day 2: _____

_____

Day 3: _____

_____

Day 4: _____

_____

Day 5: _____

_____

Day 6: _____

_____

Day 7: _____

_____

After day 7 or when you feel she's shifted into the next phase, tabulate your notes in the Weekly Note Summary

Other Points: _____

_____

Weekly Note Summary: Week 12

VOLCANO Week - Cycle 3

Start date:.................................... End date:....................................

Day	Observations about your partner and her feelings towards you	Other issues (if any)
1		
2		
3		
4		
5		
6		
7		

Mood Cycle Analysis Results

"It is wisdom to know others;
It is enlightenment to know one's self"

Lao-Tzu (6th century B.C)

Now that you've completed your three month Mood Diary, it's time to analyze the results.

These results will help you to gain insight into the specifics of your partner's 4 week mood cycle, so you'll have what you need to improve your relationship.

Let's begin:

- Firstly go to your 'Weekly Note Summaries'.

    1) RELIEF Week: weeks 1, 5 and 9

    2) LOVE Week: weeks 2, 6 and 10

    3) RESTLESS Week: weeks 3, 7 and 11

    4) VOLCANO Week: weeks 4, 8 and 12

- Next, review all your Weekly Note Summaries for each phase of her 4 week mood cycle and look for the most common reoccurring issues that have arisen over the past three months and list these feelings in the provided Mood Cycle Analysis boxes

- Then, try to understand WHY your partner's emotions and feelings manifest in this way. Write your thoughts down in the space provided

- From this emerging pattern, brainstorm some realistic coping strategies that will help you move through these feelings when they come around again. You can consult my Nature of a Woman book or audiobook for some ideas

Women and all people for that matter, have their own distinct patterns. There are *no* right or wrong answers here. This analysis is merely a snapshot of your partner's unique emotional 'wiring'.

If you are aware of what's going on for her, as well as when and *why* she feels the way she does and how this makes you feel, it will be possible to:

- Know yourself and your partner intimately

- Anticipate her emotional well being

- Change and adapt the way you respond to her, according to which phase of the 4 week mood cycle she is in

- Work with your life partner so that you can together, create a mutually respectful, understanding, forgiving and loving relationship

Example (step 4)

As an example, to be absolutely clear about how to create your Mood Cycle Analysis, I'll share some of my journal entries with you.

RELIEF Week Average Phase Duration

Cycle 1: 5 days   Cycle 2: 5 days   Cycle 3: 5 days

Total up these 3 figures: 15 days   Divide this total by 3

= Average Phase Duration: 5 days

Reoccurring Observations	Real Cause of Feelings	Coping Strategies
Cycle 1: Exhaustion, Being tired, complaining about feeling bloated	There was some bad PMS last week. There was lots of stress and she was tossing and turning all night. I think she was feeling quite physically and emotionally drained	When I see that she's obviously hormonal, I need to insist that she take some time out for herself so she has some space. This week I'll do some shopping and cooking. I'll also look after the kitchen.
Cycle 2: Guilt	Last week she said some terrible things to me. I think she's feeling really insecure and she unconsciously tried to provoke me into reacting which would have proved to her that she was 'right' me being an ogre.	This week I'm going to find the right time to talk about how saying all of that horrible stuff to me has negative consequences. I really think she needs to be made aware of this.
Cycle 3: Remorse	Now that she's moved through PMS, she's fine. She has even apologized about her behaivour. I know that these feelings last week are from her insecurities carried on from her first marriage.	This week I also need to talk to her so she understands that talking to me like that really upsets me and how It's not fair. I have to prepare her so she knows that if she get like that again I'm going to go out and give her some space.

Mood Cycle Analysis Results - RELIEF Week

Average Phase Duration

Week 1 - Cycle 1: ....   Week 5 - Cycle 2: ....   Week 9 - Cycle 3: ....

Total up these 3 figures: ....   Divide this total by 3

= Average Phase Duration: .... days

Reoccurring Observations	Real Cause of Feelings	Coping Strategies
Cycle 1:		
Cycle 2:		
Cycle 3:		

If you need more space use the 'notes' section at the end of the book.

Mood Cycle Analysis Results - LOVE Week

Average Phase Duration

Week 2 - Cycle 1: ....   Week 6 - Cycle 2: ....   Week 10 - Cycle 3: ....

Total up these 3 figures: ....   Divide this total by 3

= Average Phase Duration: .... days

Reoccurring Observations	Real Cause of Feelings	Coping Strategies
Cycle 1:		
Cycle 2:		
Cycle 3:		

If you need more space use the 'notes' section at the end of the book.

Mood Cycle Analysis Results - RESTLESS Week

Average Phase Duration

Week 3 - Cycle 1: ....   Week 7 - Cycle 2: ....   Week 11 - Cycle 3: ....

Total up these 3 figures: ....   Divide this total by 3

= Average Phase Duration: .... days

Reoccurring Observations	Real Cause of Feelings	Coping Strategies
Cycle 1:		
Cycle 2:		
Cycle 3:		

If you need more space use the 'notes' section at the end of the book.

Mood Cycle Analysis Results - VOLCANO Week

Average Phase Duration

Week 4 - Cycle 1: ....   Week 8 - Cycle 2: ....   Week 12 - Cycle 3: ....

Total up these 3 figures: ....   Divide this total by 3

= Average Phase Duration: .... days

Reoccurring Observations	Real Cause of Feelings	Coping Strategies
Cycle 1:		
Cycle 2:		
Cycle 3:		

If you need more space use the 'notes' section at the end of the book.

Moving Forward

Now that you've done the work and understand how your partner moves through her unique 4 week mood cycle, I'd like to continue to help you move forward in creating a wonderful relationship with the woman in your life.

'Nature of a Woman: Survival Skills for MEN book and audiobook'

My book and audio book of the same title, is available from this link

www.survivalskillsformen.com

Survival Skills Men's Group

When it comes to having problems at home, it's quite cathartic to hear that you are not alone in finding it difficult to understand and deal with an emotional partner.

My aim is to help as many guys as possible develop their Survival Skills and thrive in their relationship with a woman.

To that end, I also invite you to join my men's group on Facebook called: TheSS4MCircle where we can share stories, discuss issues as well as brainstorm strategies to build and maintain a successful relationship

https://www.facebook.com/groups/TheSS4MCircle/

Bonus Content

Once you've read this book access my free bonus content:

'3 Tips for When Your Partner is Crying (for no reason)'

This short video will give you 3 practical strategies and tips if you are in a situation where your partner is either upset or mad and you don't know what to do.

'Mind Clearing Breathing Exercise'

This audio training will help prepare you as well as develop the correct mindset for journaling. This breathing technique can also help you in any other area of your life when you feel tense, apprehensive or upset.

To access your bonus content please use this link:

www.survivalskillsformen.com/bonus/

Resource Page

I have a few links to websites, some free bonus content, as well as some downloads and further reading.

To keep things simple, I've compiled them all onto one page. To access these resources please use this link:

www.survivalskillsformen.com/resources

About the Author

From humble beginnings working in amongst the rough and tumble of dockyards, mining camps and the oil industry, Gary lived, worked and played with some of the hardest and toughest people in our society before embarking on a career in the entertainment industry.

Gary is also a 6th Dan black belt Master Instructor and currently owns and operates a successful Martial Arts school.

Gary lives in Sydney, Australia, with his wife and business partner Christine. They are passionately focused on empowering people to meet their potential through the Martial Arts and Yoga.

They also work together to produce books in the personal development genre.

Notes

Notes

Notes

Notes

www.ingramcontent.com/pod-product-compliance
Lightning Source LLC
Chambersburg PA
CBHW060518300426
44112CB00017B/2718